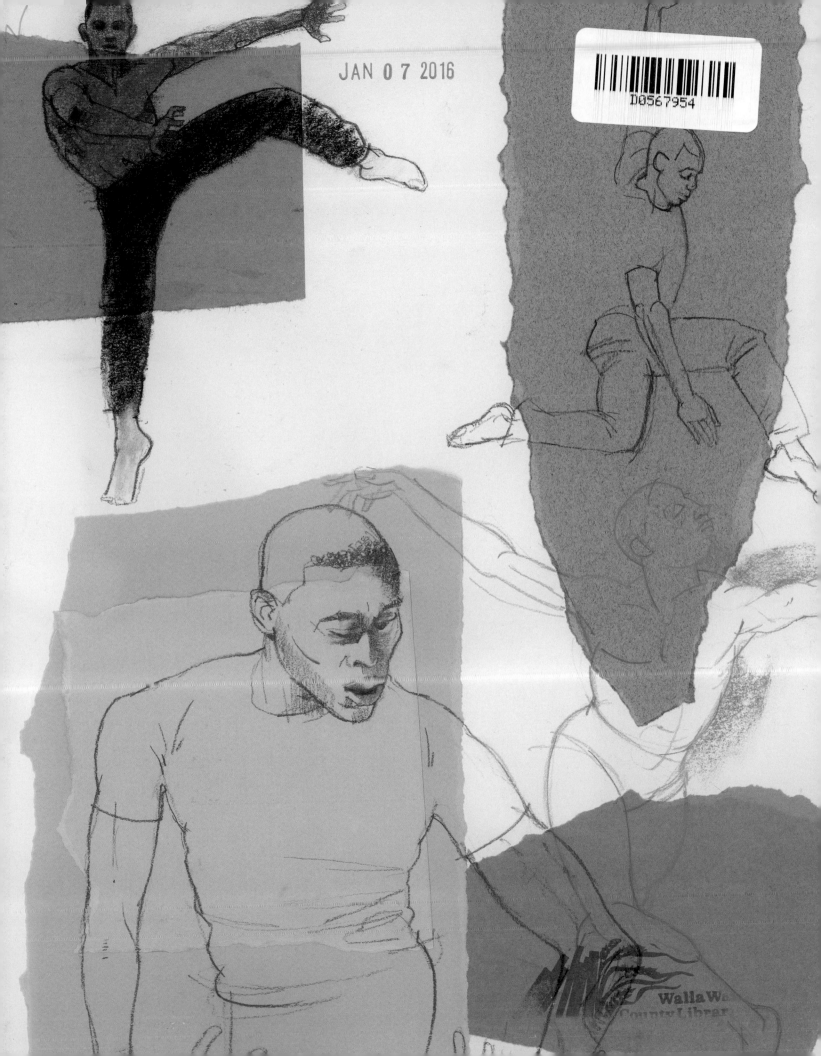

MY STORY,

For Cheryl, Sharyn, and Melaney
in honor of all the dance floors we've shared
—L. C.-R.

For Alvin Ailey, Judith Jamison, and Robert Battle
and modern dancers everywhere
—J. E. R.

SIMON & SCHUSTER BOOKS FOR YOUNG READERS
An imprint of Simon & Schuster Children's Publishing Division
1230 Avenue of the Americas, New York, New York 10020
Text copyright © 2015 by Lesa Cline-Ransome
Illustrations copyright © 2015 by James Ransome
All rights reserved, including the right of reproduction in whole or in part in any form.
SIMON & SCHUSTER BOOKS FOR YOUNG READERS is a trademark of Simon & Schuster, Inc.
For information about special discounts for bulk purchases, please contact Simon & Schuster Special Sales
at 1-866-506-1949 or business@simonandschuster.com.
The Simon & Schuster Speakers Bureau can bring authors to your live event.
For more information or to book an event, contact the Simon & Schuster Speakers Bureau
at 1-866-248-3049 or visit our website at www.simonspeakers.com.
Book design by Laurent Linn
The text for this book is set in Warnock Pro.
The illustrations for this book are rendered in pastel.
Manufactured in the United States of America
0915 LAK
10 9 8 7 6 5 4 3 2 1
Library of Congress Cataloging-in-Publication Data
Cline-Ransome, Lesa.
My story, my dance : Robert Battle's journey to Alvin Ailey / Lesa Cline-Ransome ;
illustrated by James E. Ransome.
pages cm
"A Paula Wiseman Book."
ISBN 978-1-4814-2221-5 (hardcover) — ISBN 978-1-4814-2222-2 (ebook)
1. Battle, Robert, 1972– 2. Choreographers—United States—Biography.
3. Dancers—United States—Biography. 4. Alvin Ailey American Dance Theater.
I. Ransome, James, illustrator. II. Title.
GV1785.B3487C55 2015
792.82092—dc23
[B]
2014007181

first
edition

MY DANCE

ROBERT BATTLE'S JOURNEY TO ALVIN AILEY

written by
LESA CLINE-RANSOME

illustrated by
JAMES E. RANSOME

with a foreword by
ROBERT BATTLE

A Paula Wiseman Book

SIMON & SCHUSTER
BOOKS FOR YOUNG READERS
New York London Toronto Sydney New Delhi

FOREWORD

When I was growing up in the Liberty City neighborhood of Miami, I would climb a big mango tree in the backyard. The tree had been there long before me (and is still there), and something about it made me feel small and gave me perspective. There I could listen to my inner compass and think. It was always important for me to have an image of myself in relationship to the world and my broader community. At the tip of my tongue was always the question "Who am I?"

When I first saw *Revelations*, in some ways it felt like something I had already imagined as a child. After seeing the Alvin Ailey performers onstage who looked like me and my family, I began to be able to answer the question of who I was and where I fit in. Mr. Ailey created *Revelations* as a way to tell both his own story and the story of the African American community, and to demonstrate that dance was for everybody. He internalized his experiences and turned them into dances that celebrate the human spirit. I realized that creating a dance embodies everything that I learned sitting up in that tree: It is the process of visualizing and exploring one's place in the world.

It is my hope that my story will encourage young people to dream and find their own places in the world through art. I want them to understand that success comes from imagination and hard work and support from those around them. I want to thank my great-aunt and great-uncle, Anna and Willie Horne; my mother, Dessie Williams; my family; my teachers; and, of course, Alvin Ailey and Judith Jamison, as well as all the others who have helped guide me on my journey. And my heartfelt thanks to everyone at Simon & Schuster, especially Lesa Cline-Ransome and James E. Ransome, for turning my story into a beautiful book.

There couldn't be a greater honor than leading Alvin Ailey American Dance Theater, the company that inspired me: I have the opportunity to inspire others in the same way that I was inspired, and to move others to imagine their own worlds, their own dances. Dance is a metaphor for how we get through life. It's about timing, it's about daring, it's about grace, it's about intensity, it's about overcoming difficult steps—but then, finally, it's about finding joy.

—ROBERT BATTLE

It was a blue sky Sunday on the day he was born.
Hot Jacksonville sun greeted a brown-skinned, bright-eyed,
bowlegged boy named Robert.

It was August 1972, and folks headed out to church service, fanning themselves to cool down in the Florida heat. But Robert's uncle Willie and aunt Anna made their way across town to meet their brand-new baby nephew. Times were tough for Robert's mama, Marie. When Robert was, as Uncle Willie described, "no bigger than a loaf of bread," he and Aunt Anna took Robert in.

When Aunt Anna became sick, the three of them packed up and headed south to Miami, to be closer to Anna and Willie's daughter, Robert's cousin Dessie. In a little house in the Liberty City neighborhood, Dessie was waiting with a down-home family welcome. Dessie taught English, wrote poetry, played piano in the church, and loved Robert like her own.

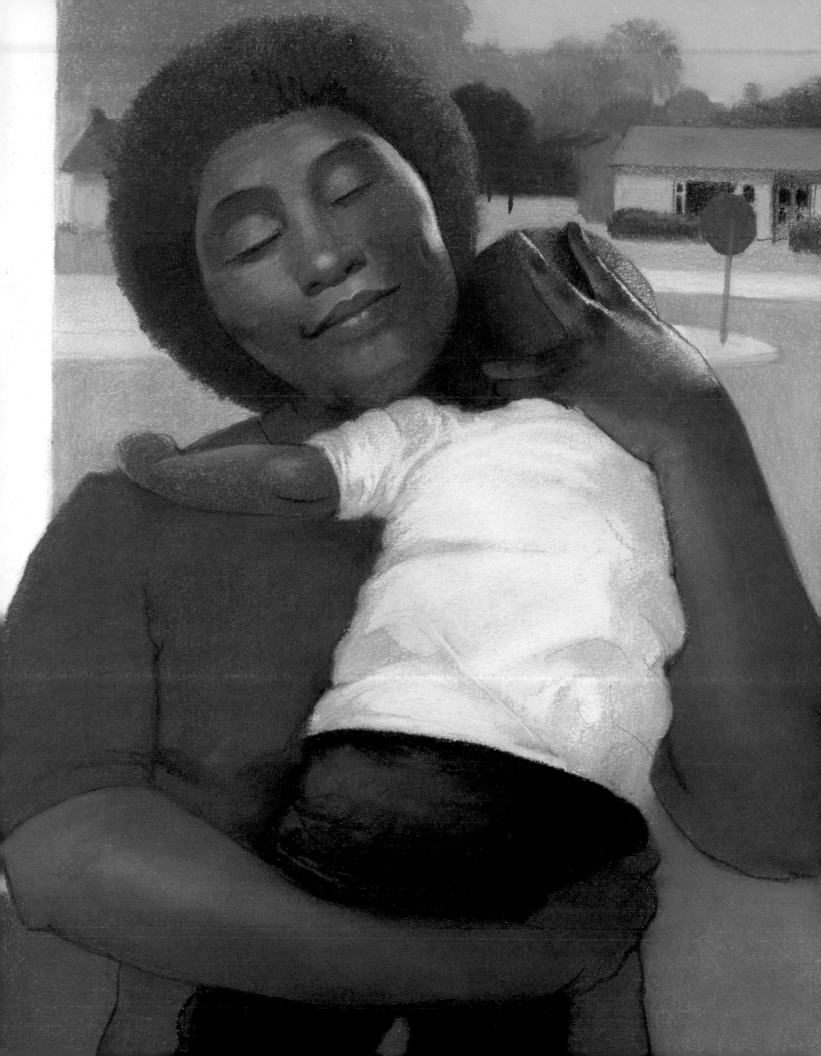

Out on the front porch, when his mama Dessie practiced with her performance group, the Afro Americans, Robert watched. When they sang spirituals, Robert hummed along. And when they recited the poetry of Mari Evans and Maya Angelou, Robert listened. On his mama Dessie's rehearsal days, there was no place else he'd rather be.

On Sundays in the choir stand, Robert sang like a bird in his sweet soprano, while mama Dessie played hymns on the piano.

This is my story
This is my song
Praising my savior
All the day long

After service and Sunday supper, Robert sat at the piano and filled his house with music. He was too shy to play in front of Miss Juanita, his piano teacher. But when he was alone, his fingers glided across the keys, as he happily made up his own songs.

In the evenings, the heavy metal braces he wore to straighten his legs slowed Robert to a stop. For years, Robert felt the pain and heard the clank of metal whenever he moved his legs. Trying to walk, he fell down time and again, until finally his legs got straighter and stronger.

When he was six, his braces came off, and Robert strode onto the pulpit of Wactor Temple AME Zion Church dressed in a fine Easter suit. He looked out and saw his mama Dessie and uncle Willie and the faces of everyone in his church family. He took a deep breath and recited the poem his mama Dessie had taught him.

My name is Robert Battle
And I stand six feet tall
And I just came to say
Happy Easter Day

"Amen," said the congregation when Robert returned to his seat, and he blushed with pride. In that moment, Robert knew that being onstage gave him a confidence he never thought he had.

Back at home, his living room floor became a stage, lit with the smiles of his uncle Willie and mama Dessie.

Robert soft-shoed like Fred Astaire and moonwalked like Michael Jackson. *"The world is a stage,"* he sang in his best Broadway voice, *"the stage is a world of entertainment!"*

Outside the comfort of church and the haven of home, Robert was called names that hurt worse than his leg braces ever had. His mama Dessie wanted him to be safe on Liberty City streets, so at age twelve Robert began to study martial arts. He spent hours practicing katas, his arms and legs slicing through the air, his feet stepping and stomping.

Now when he walked the streets of Liberty City, Robert felt safer, imagining he was a black-belt warrior like Bruce Lee. He found calm in the discipline and courage in his growing strength. But the best part was that karate sounded like music and felt like dancing.

"Be that what you is. Don't try to be that what you ain't," his uncle Willie said when Robert told him and his mama Dessie he wanted to dance. And not just like Gene Kelly and Bill "Bojangles" Robinson. He wanted to dance like the kids from his school who practiced turns and positions. He wanted to dance ballet.

At thirteen, Robert nervously waited for his first lesson to begin. He was much older than many of those in his class.

Loose and limber from karate, Robert's lean frame easily maneuvered through the warm-ups at the African Heritage Cultural Arts Center on Miami's Twenty-Second Avenue. At the barre, Robert glided through his pliés, relevés, port de bras, and coupés. When the music began to play, Robert's heart began to race.

As a freshman at Miami Northwestern High School, Robert signed up for the after-school dance program. He'd been dancing for two years at the arts center, and he knew that most dancers started training before they were five years old. In his classes, Robert was the first to arrive and the last to leave. He knew he had a lot of catching up to do.

Miss Munez, a former New York City Ballet dancer and a partner in Miami's Caracas Ballet, strode into the dance studio, small and serious. As she began their first lesson, something about the tall young man in the back row caught her eye. Robert had something special.

She filled his arms with dance magazines and books on ballet. On days off she made Robert come in for private lessons, and on Saturdays she drove him to extra classes at the Ballet Academy of Miami. He didn't have time to moan about his aching muscles and groan about wearing tights.

During a break, Robert finally got up the nerve to ask the question that had been on his mind.

"Do you think I can be the first black Baryshnikov?" he asked shyly, hoping to someday perform like the famed Russian ballet dancer he'd seen on television and in magazines.

"You can be whatever you want to be," Miss Munez told him,
and turned the music on to resume his lesson.

Robert boarded the bus with his dance class. They were on their way to see a dance company performing in Miami Beach. Once they were settled in their seats and the lights were dimmed, Robert's eyes never left the stage. In piece after piece, dancers in all shades of brown moved powerfully, gracefully across the stage. And when the *Revelations* finale began, they all moved as one to a mournful spiritual.

Rock-a my soul in the bosom of Abraham
Rock-a my soul in the bosom of Abraham
Oh, rock-a my soul.

From his seat Robert felt their pain, their joy, their sorrow and hope. Onstage he saw his mama Dessie, Uncle Willie and Aunt Anna, Miss Juanita, the members of his congregation at Wactor Temple AME. In the Alvin Ailey dance company, Robert saw his past and his future, and he saw himself.

The New World School of the Arts in Miami was holding auditions for high school students, and Robert was not going.

"I'm gonna stay here with you," he told Miss Munez, feeling she was the best dance teacher he could ever have.

Robert finished his rehearsal, but Miss Munez was waiting.

"You're going to the New World School of the Arts and I don't want to talk about it."

They worked day and night on his audition piece, perfecting his jumps and turns, and when the day finally arrived, Robert worried he'd forget everything he learned. When Robert received an acceptance letter, he felt as light as he had when his leg braces first came off.

During his two years at New World, Robert not only grew in inches to a full six feet tall, but he also grew in technique with the help of his teacher Gerri Houlihan. Gently, she encouraged and taught and pushed Robert's dancing until his movements felt as natural to him as breathing. In the New World dance studio, soaking in music and dripping with sweat, he'd never felt more at home.

"You take care of yourself, boy. Remember that head is not just a place to hang a hat," Uncle Willie instructed. Robert was going to miss his family, but he knew it was time to go. In his final year at New World, he'd auditioned for and received a full scholarship to the school he'd only read about in dance magazines. His mama Dessie sat in the car, waiting to take him to the airport. Robert was off to New York to dance at the Juilliard School.

Filled with the world's most promising actors, musicians, and dancers, Juilliard sat between Amsterdam and Broadway on West Sixty-Fifth Street. In August of 1990, Robert arrived loaded with suitcases and fears about whether all the training he received back in Florida would be enough here in New York.

When he began creating his own dances, he listened over and over to critiques and criticisms. But from his teachers Bessie Schönberg, Elizabeth Keen, and Benjamin Harkavy he learned that dance was a way to tell his own story.

Robert told his story in the pieces he created and in his own dance performances. His choreography won the Princess Grace and Martha Hill awards. When he graduated from Juilliard and was invited to join the Parsons Dance Company in New York City, he brought with him pieces of home and memories of family. He choreographed *The Hunt*, where dancers kicked and chopped just like he had long ago in karate class. *In/Side* captured all his fears as a young boy in Liberty City. And in *Strange Humors* the dancers' falls told the story of all the nights his leg braces had made it difficult to walk.

In 2001 Robert began his own dance company, Battleworks. Soon his new company was performing to rave reviews from state to state. Judith Jamison was the artistic director of Alvin Ailey American Dance Theater when she saw Robert's *Mood Indigo*, and she wanted her own company to feature it. Robert's future lay with Ailey.

On a blue sky summer day, ten years and eleven dances later, Robert began as the new artistic director of Alvin Ailey.

As Robert stepped onstage at the crowded theater on July 1, 2011, he looked out and imagined the faces of his mama Dessie, Uncle Willie and Aunt Anna, Miss Juanita, the congregation at Wactor Temple AME, Miss Munez, Gerri Houlihan, his Juilliard teachers, and Judith Jamison. In the audience he saw his past, his present, and his future, and he saw himself.

Robert stepped forward, opened his arms to the audience, and welcomed each and every one, like family.

Acknowledgments

The publisher gratefully acknowledges the inspiration and cooperation of the Ailey and Ailey II dance companies during the making of this book. Special thanks to Christopher Zunner, director of public relations of Alvin Ailey American Dance Theater, for his invaluable help. And thanks to Nick Vergoth for the spark that made this book happen.

Author's Note

"The best works of art are the ones that are the most personal."
—ALVIN AILEY

For years during the holiday season, my husband, James, and I travelled with our children from our home in upstate New York to New York City. We made all the usual stops—the Christmas tree at Rockefeller Center, the window displays along Fifth Avenue, an early dinner at a kid-friendly restaurant. But the highlight of our trip was our visit to New York City Center to see Alvin Ailey American Dance Theater. With all four of our children bundled up against the cold, walking city blocks, trudging onto train platforms, hailing taxis, often arriving just as the curtain went up, my husband and I often wondered if it was worth it. But once we settled in, the rewards of our long journey came to life onstage. The six of us were transported and transformed by the Alvin Ailey dancers. Our children leaned forward in their seats, eyes wide, not wanting to miss a single moment of the drama unfolding onstage. Each dance had special meaning, but for me, the energy and spirit of *Revelations* made me proud of my African American heritage and prouder still to be a black woman. Like Robert Battle, I saw a piece of myself onstage.

When dear friends Andrea Davis Pinkney and Brian Pinkney wrote and illustrated the picture book *Alvin Ailey* nearly two decades ago, I, like many others, was struck by the story of the creative talents and passion of a man who changed the world of modern dance.

When I was approached by my editors Paula Wiseman and Sylvie Frank to write the story of Robert Battle, I agreed before I realized that though I'd written many biographies of prominent people in history, I hadn't yet written one about a contemporary figure, let alone a contemporary figure in dance. While I have always enjoyed dance, it's been from a viewer's perspective. Through my research and attending countless dance performances, I discovered that the life of a dancer is not an easy one. Given the required hours of daily practice, I think the true beauty of dance lies in the act of making difficult movements appear simple and graceful.

What an honor it was to write about Robert Battle, a man whose own personal history is closely aligned with Ailey's. Upon meeting Robert, I was touched by his compassion, humor, and integrity, all the elements seen in many of the works he has choreographed and commissioned. Over lunch, at a restaurant near the Ailey studios, Robert shared many stories of his childhood in Miami, the overwhelming support of his family, community, and teachers. Not all of those wonderful stories made their way into this biography, but I certainly did my best to infuse these pages with the essence of Robert's heart and passion.

As the newly minted artistic director of a dance institution, he faces the unique challenge of telling his own story while preserving the legacy of Alvin Ailey. Though the two never met (Alvin Ailey passed away in 1989, when Robert was seventeen years old), both were close friends of former artistic director Judith Jamison, who was selected by Alvin Ailey and who in turn chose Robert Battle as her successor. Both Ailey and Battle were born in the South, grew up in the church, admired Fred Astaire, studied martial arts, began dancing in their early teens, and saw their first dance performances on class trips. Most importantly, both men's sense of history, passion, and purpose are demonstrated in their brilliant artistic visions for the Alvin Ailey American Dance Theater.

—LESA CLINE-RANSOME

Illustrator's Note

Depicting dance in pastels has a long tradition in art. Two of my favorite artists, Edgar Degas and Robert Heindel, were well known for their pastel drawings of ballet dancers. Inspired by that tradition, I, too, chose pastels to capture the color, movement, and fluidity of the Alvin Ailey dancers. When I had the opportunity to attend rehearsals and performances, I was further inspired by the hard work, tireless repetition, creativity, and collaboration among dancers and choreographers.

My Story, My Dance combines both past and present inspirations for my own contemporary vision of the beauty of dance and Robert Battle, the man who is creating his own artistic traditions for Alvin Ailey.

—JAMES E. RANSOME

Bibliography

ARTICLES

Acocella, Joan. "New Move: Alvin Ailey at City Center." *New Yorker*, December 19, 2011.

de la Peña, Matthew. "Robert Battle Interview." *Time Out Chicago*. Time Out, March 6, 2013.
http://www.timeout.com/chicago/theater/robert-battle-interview.

Hollingsworth, Annie. "Miami's Robert Battle Brings Alvin Ailey to the Arsht Center." *Miami New Times*, February 23, 2012.
http://www.miaminewtimes.com/2012-02-23/culture/miami-s-robert-battle-brings-alvin-ailey-to-the-arsht-center.

Johnson, Robert. "Robert Battle to Lead Alvin Ailey American Dance Theater." NJ.com, April 29, 2010.
http://www.nj.com/entertainment/arts/index.ssf/2010/04/robert_battle_to_lead_alvin_ai.html.

Kourlas, Gia. "For New Ailey Leader, It's All in the Family." *New York Times*, May 7, 2010.
http://www.nytimes.com/2010/05/09/arts/dance/09battle.html?_r=0.

Perron, Wendy. "Robert Battle: The First Season." *Dance Magazine*, December 2011.
http:/dancemagazine.com/issues/december-2011/Robert-Battle-The-First-Season-expanded-version.

Wildalice1. "Alvin Ailey - Revelations." Studymode.com, January 2013.
http://www.studymode.com/essays/Alvin-Ailey-Revelations-1338164.html.

VIDEO AND RADIO

Alvin Ailey American Dance Theater. "Ailey Classics." YouTube video, 4:14. November 27, 2012.
http://www.youtube.com/watch?v=vXiqAshNlzw.

Alvin Ailey American Dance Theater. "Alvin Ailey's Revelations." YouTube video, 2:52. February 17, 2012.
https://www.youtube.com/watch?v=LZuBFz6WYfs&list=UUg9o2fgvhIPlow5gi0sc-1w.

Arts Guild, The. "Interview with Robert Battle." YouTube video, 8:52. February 3, 2012.
http://www.youtube.com/watch?v=2ap0DovR0mM.

City.Ballet. AOL On Originals Web series, 2013. http://on.aol.com/show/cityballet-517887470/episode/517995636.

Dance Consortium. "Robert Battle Interview, Alvin Ailey American Dance Theater." YouTube video, 4:07. October 4, 2010.
http://www.youtube.com/watch?v=WJuRgrF6u7Q.

Dance Enthusiast, The. "New York Dance Up Close: Alvin Ailey American Dance Theater 'LIFT' Rehearsal Process." YouTube video, 3:11. December 3, 2013. http://www.youtube.com/watch?v=iROkBdjS2EA.

"Dancer-Choreographer Robert Battle." *Tavis Smiley*. PBS Video. April 29, 2011. http://video.pbs.org/video/1902535964.

"Falling and Rising with Robert Battle." *CNN Profiles*. CNN Radio. February 22, 2013.
http://cnnradio.cnn.com/2013/02/22/cnn-profiles-falling-and-rising-with-robert-battle.

Website

Alvin Ailey American Dance Theater
http://www.alvinailey.org

Further Reading

Allen, Debbie. *Dancing in the Wings*. New York: Puffin, 2003.

Copeland, Misty. *Firebird: Ballerina Misty Copeland Shows a Young Girl How to Dance Like a Firebird*.
Illustrated by Christopher Myers. New York: Putnam, 2014.

Dempsey, Kristy. *A Dance Like Starlight: One Ballerina's Dream*. Illustrated by Floyd Cooper. New York: Philomel, 2014.

Dillon, Leo and Diane. *Rap A Tap Tap: Here's Bojangles—Think of That!* New York: Blue Sky Press, 2002.

Greenberg, Jan, and Sandra Jordan. *Ballet for Martha: Making Appalachian Spring*. New York: Roaring Brook Press, 2010.

Gruska, Denise. *The Only Boy in Ballet*. Illustrated by Amy Wummer. Layton, UT: Gibbs Smith, 2007.

Jones, Bill T. and Susan Kuklin. *Dance! With Bill T. Jones*. New York: Disney-Hyperion, 1998.

Pinkney, Andrea Davis. *Alvin Ailey*. Illustrated by Brian Pinkney. New York: Disney-Hyperion, 1995.

Reich, Susanna. *José!: Born to Dance*. Illustrated by Raúl Colón. New York: Simon & Schuster, 2005.